Intermediate English Dialogues: Speak American English Like a Native Speaker with these Phrases, Idioms, & Expressions

Jackie Bolen

www.eslspeaking.org

Copyright © 2021 by Jackie Bolen

All rights reserved. No part of this publication may be reproduced, distributed, or transmitted in any form or by any means, including photocopying, recording or other electronic or mechanical means without the prior written permission of the publisher, except in the case of brief quotations in critical reviews and certain other non-commercial uses permitted by copyright law. For permission requests, write to the publisher/author at the following address: Jackie Bolen: jb.business.online@gmail.com.

Table of Contents

About the Author: Jackie Bolen 4
Introduction to Intermediate English Dialogues 5
Running Late 6
The Ice Cream Shop 8
Sit Tight 10
House Hunting 12
Deciding How to Get Somewhere 14
Weather Forecast 16
Stuck in a Traffic Jam 18
From Dawn Till Dusk 20
Hit the Sack 22
Save me a Seat 24
At the Farmer's Market 26
Save the Environment 28
Supermarket Strategy 30
Eating Habits 32
The Last Straw 34
Buying a New Computer 36
Good With Computers 38
Played Soccer 40
Weekend Plans #1 42
Weekend Plans #2 44
Bite the Bullet 46
Doing Chores 48
Surf the Web 50
How to Split Chores 52
Apply for University 54
No Pain No Gain 56
Vacation Plans 58
Break a Leg 60
At the Movie Theater 62
A Suspicious Person 64
You Can't Judge a Book by Its Cover 66
The New Guy 68
Feeling Under the Weather 70
Talking About an Accident 72
Talking About the Weather 74
Buttering Me Up 76
Talking About a New Phone 78
Help With Moving 80
Bumping into Someone 82
The Sleepover 84
Before You Go 86

About the Author: Jackie Bolen

I taught English in South Korea for 10 years to every level and type of student. I've taught every age from kindergarten kids to adults. Most of my time has centered around teaching at two universities: five years at a science and engineering school in Cheonan, and four years at a major university in Busan where I taught upper-level classes for students majoring in English. In my spare time, you can usually find me outside surfing, biking, hiking, or snowshoeing. I now live in Vancouver, Canada.

In case you were wondering what my academic qualifications are, I hold a Master of Arts in Psychology. During my time in Korea, I completed both the Cambridge CELTA and DELTA certification programs. With the combination of almost ten years teaching ESL/EFL learners of all ages and levels, and the more formal teaching qualifications I've obtained, I have a solid foundation on which to offer advice to English learners.

I truly hope that you find this book useful. I would love it if you sent me an email with any questions or feedback that you might have.

Jackie Bolen (www.jackiebolen.com)

Twitter: @bolen_jackie

Email: jb.business.online@gmail.com

You might also be interested in this book: Advanced English Conversation Dialogues. It has hundreds of helpful English idioms and expressions. You can find it wherever you like to buy books. Learn to speak more fluently in American English.

Introduction to Intermediate English Dialogues

Welcome to this book designed to help you expand your knowledge of American English. My goal is to help you speak and write more fluently.

Let's face it, English can be difficult to master, even for the best students. In this book, you'll find dialogues that are ideal for intermediate-level students.

The best way to learn new vocabulary is in context.

To get the most bang for your buck, be sure to do the following:

- Review frequently.

- Try to use some of the phrases and expressions in real life.

- Don't be nervous about making mistakes. That's how you'll get better at English!

- Consider studying with a friend so you can help each other stay motivated.

- Use a notebook and write down new words, idioms, expressions, etc. that you run across. Review frequently so that they stay fresh in your mind.

- Be sure to answer the questions at the end of each dialogue. I recommend trying to do this from memory. No peeking!

- I recommend doing one dialogue a day. This will be more beneficial than finishing the entire book in a week or two.

Good luck and I wish you well on your journey to becoming more proficient with American English.

Running Late

Zeke wants to let Sid know that he is running late.

Zeke: Sid. Hi. So sorry but I'm **running late** and can't meet you for dinner at 6:30.

Sid: Oh, okay. You're late **once in a blue moon**! I don't mind. What time do you think you'll get here?

Zeke: By 7:00 at the latest, I think. There was a **car crash** ahead of me on the highway.

Sid: Oh no! Is it cleared?

Zeke: It will be soon. It looks like the police are finishing up now and traffic is moving slowly. Hopefully, we'll be **rolling soon**.

Sid: Sure. See you when you get here. **No rush**. I'll just have a glass of wine to **kill time**. It isn't terrible, to say the least.

Zeke: Can't complain about that, right? Thanks for understanding. I appreciate it. Oh, and it's my treat so **order a bottle**, okay?

Vocabulary

Running late: Being behind schedule.

Once in a blue moon: Not often.

Car crash: Accident.

Rolling soon: Will start moving shortly.

No rush: Don't hurry.

Kill time: Do something to fill time.

Order a bottle: Get a bottle of wine, instead of just a glass at a restaurant.

Practice

Fill in the blanks with the correct word or phrase.

1. Hey Ted, I'm sorry but I'm _____.
2. I'd love to see the report but it's _____. I can wait.
3. I only smoke _____.
4. There's a _____ on Whyte Ave. Let's find a different route.
5. I usually watch Netflix when I have to _____.
6. Let's _____ for the whole table.
7. Get ready! We'll be _____ on all these new contracts.

Answers

1. running late
2. no rush
3. once in a blue moon
4. car crash
5. kill time
6. order a bottle
7. rolling soon

The Ice Cream Shop

Mandy and Todd are deciding what kind of ice cream to get.

Mandy: There are so many choices here! I'm **like a kid in a candy shop**.

Todd: They don't call it 99 **scoops** for nothing! **What's your fancy?**

Mandy: I know it's boring but I usually **go for** the same thing every time. I get **a double**: cookies & cream and rainbow sherbet.

Todd: Those are **classics** for sure! Can't go wrong with them. **Sticking with** what you love. Not a bad strategy at all.

Mandy: What do you like?

Todd: I like to **mix it up** and get something different every time. I think I'll go for the salted caramel. I'm sure I'll have some regret when I see the ones you got though!

Vocabulary

Like a kid in a candy shop: Feeling very happy! Lots of good things to choose from.

Scoops: Refers to ice cream balls.

What's your fancy?: A kind of old-fashioned way to ask, "What do you like/want?"

A double: 2 scoops of ice cream.

Classics: The usual things. Not new and trendy.

Sticking with: Not choosing something new; going with the familiar.

Mix it up: Change something; choose a new thing.

Practice

Fill in the blanks with the correct word or phrase.

1. All these new cars? I'm _____.
2. Why don't we _____ and get Chinese tonight?
3. I prefer _____ to new releases.
4. How many _____ are you going to get?
5. What do you think about _____ this contractor for next year?
6. _____. I'm thinking of going with pepperoni and mushroom.
7. I'd like _____ please: chocolate and French vanilla.

Answers

1. like a kid in a candy shop
2. mix it up
3. classics
4. scoops
5. sticking with
6. What's your fancy?
7. a double

Sit Tight

Jason and Linda are talking about when to leave to get the train.

Jason: Hey, let's get moving! **Time is money.**

Linda: Sit tight. I need to grab a few things before we go.

Jason: Come on. We have to get to the train station on time. I hate always being the **bad guy** about stuff like this.

Linda: Well, to be fair, you've been as **clear as mud** about what time we needed to leave. Traffic won't be as bad as you think.

Jason: There are always **traffic jams** at this time. Let's **get a move on.**

Linda: Okay, I'll be ready **in the blink of an eye**. Stop bugging me!

Vocabulary

Sit tight: Wait patiently and don't take any action right now.

Clear as mud: Confusing or not easy to understand.

Time is money: To try to get someone to work faster or more efficiently.

Traffic jams: When cars aren't moving quickly because it's busy.

Get a move on: Hurry up.

Bad guy: Someone who always has bad news/enforces a rule.

In the blink of an eye: In a short amount of time.

Practice

Fill in the blanks with the correct word or phrase.

1. If you leave after 8 am, there will be lots of _____.
2. Let's _____. I don't want to be late for school.
3. I try to always remember that _____.
4. I had a terrible teacher in high school. His explanations were as _____.
5. _____ while I check and see what time the movie starts.
6. I hate to be the _____ but you need to get it together or you're going to get fired.
7. Don't miss the eclipse. It'll happen _____.

Answers

1. traffic jams
2. get a move on
3. time is money
4. clear as mud
5. Sit tight
6. bad guy
7. in the blink of an eye

House Hunting

Craig and Ted are talking about buying a new place.

Craig: What are you up to **this weekend**?

Ted: I'm going **house hunting**.

Craig: How exciting! It's almost impossible to save up a **down payment** with how expensive rent is in **this town**.

Ted: No kidding. I'll never be able to **pay off my mortgage**. I barely scraped together enough for a 10% down payment.

Craig: Well, let me know if you need **help moving**.

Vocabulary

This weekend: Saturday and Sunday coming up.

House hunting: Looking for a house to buy or rent, usually buying.

Down payment: A large amount of money required up-front for purchasing a house.

This town: The city you're currently in.

No kidding: You're not joking.

Pay off my mortgage: Finish paying off a bank loan for a house.

Help moving: Help to move from an old home to a new one.

Practice

Fill in the blanks with the correct word or phrase.

1. Let me know if you need _____. I have a truck.
2. I'm planning on going to the hockey game _____.
3. It's very difficult to buy a house in _____ as they're very expensive.
4. _____. That's amazing news.
5. The _____ will need to be at least 10% of the listing price.
6. Oh, you're going _____? What areas are you looking at?
7. I plan to _____ in 10 years.

Answers

1. help moving
2. this weekend
3. this town
4. no kidding
5. down payment
6. house hunting
7. pay off my mortgage

Deciding How to Get Somewhere

Bob and Keith are talking about how to get downtown for a concert.

Keith: I'm **counting down the minutes** until the concert. I'm **pumped up** about it! Where is it? And, it's at 8:30, right?

Bob: It's at The Orpheum as far as I know. Let's check though...yeah the Orpheum and it starts at 9:00.

Keith: Parking **costs a pretty penny** downtown. What about **catching the subway** there instead of driving?

Bob: That's good for getting there but it stops running at 11:30 I think. We might have to Uber home.

Keith: That's fine with me although that **costs an arm and a leg** too from downtown to the **suburbs**.

Bob: It's okay. I'm not **flush with cash** but I did just get my monthly bonus. I'll pay for it.

Vocabulary

Counting down the minutes: Impatiently waiting for something to come.

Pumped up: Excited about something.

Costs a pretty penny: Is expensive.

Catching the subway: Taking the subway.

Costs an arm and a leg: Is expensive.

Suburbs: Communities outside the city limits.

Flush with cash: Lots of money at this exact time.

Practice

Fill in the blanks with the correct word or phrase.

1. Honestly, I'm _____ until the school year ends.
2. I don't like living in the _____ but it's way cheaper.
3. What time are we _____?
4. I'm _____ about this new video game.
5. It _____ to buy a house in Vancouver.
6. Are you sure you want to buy it? I didn't think you were _____.

Answers

1. counting down the minutes
2. suburbs
3. catching the subway
4. pumped up
5. costs a pretty penny/costs an arm and a leg
6. flush with cash

Weather Forecast

Ted and Lindsay are talking about the weather.

Ted: What's the **weather forecast** looking like this weekend? We should get out for a hike.

Lindsay: Let me check. Clear skies on Saturday but **scattered showers** on Sunday. **Hot and humid** both days.

Ted: If we're going to go to Mount Hood, we need to be **prepared for anything**. It can go from calm to **gale-force winds** so quickly.

Lindsay: That happened last time I was there. Just **light rain** at first and then the **storm clouds** rolled in and there were **wind gusts** of more than 100 km/h.

Vocabulary

Weather forecast: Prediction of future weather.

Let me check: Give me a minute to find the answer to something.

Clear skies: Not cloudy.

Scattered showers: Rain that is on and off.

Hot and humid: Muggy.

Prepared for anything: Ready to face any situation.

Gale-force winds: Very strong wind.

Light rain: Not raining heavily.

Storm clouds: Clouds that may produce rain, snow, hail, thunder, etc.

Wind gusts: Bursts of wind after periods of relative calm.

Practice

Fill in the blanks with the correct word or phrase.

1. There will be _____ of more than 150 km/hour today.
2. _____ at night usually means good weather the next day.
3. It's so _____. I just want to sit next to a pool.
4. You have to be _____ with this job.
5. I'm not sure if we have that in stock. _____.
6. There are some serious _____ over there. I think we should turn around.
7. The forecast showed some _____. Don't forget your umbrella.
8. What's the _____ for Japan this week? I need to know how to pack for my trip.
9. I know it doesn't seem like it, but _____ are not ideal when sailing.

Answers

1. wind gusts
2. clear skies
3. hot and humid
4. prepared for anything
5. let me check
6. storm clouds
7. scattered showers/light rain
8. weather forecast
9. gale-force winds

Stuck in a Traffic Jam

Richard is stuck in a traffic jam and telling Linda that he'll be late for their appointment.

Richard: Linda? Hi. Sorry, I'm going to be late for our **coffee date**. There's a **traffic jam** somewhere up ahead. We're crawling along at a **snail's pace**.

Linda: Oh no. What time will you be here?

Richard: It's **impossible to predict**. There's a lot of traffic. I'll be as fast as I can.

Linda: Okay. Keep me updated, please. I need to leave in about an hour to pick up my kids from school.

Richard: I didn't know you needed to leave at a specific time. I'll **keep you updated.**

Linda: Sure. **Better late than never**! I was **in the same boat** yesterday meeting my husband.

Vocabulary

Coffee date: Meeting with someone over coffee. May, or may not be a romantic date.

Traffic jam: Cars that aren't moving quickly because of an accident or heavy traffic up ahead.

Snail's pace: Very slow.

Impossible to predict: Unable to give an exact time, answer, etc.

Keep you updated: Give me information as you know it.

Better late than never: It's better to do something not on time than not at all.

In the same boat: Experiencing the same thing.

Practice

Fill in the blanks with the correct word or phrase.

1. There's a big _____ up ahead. Let's take another route.
2. It was due 3 weeks ago but _____.
3. I hope Toronto will win the Stanley Cup but it's _____.
4. Everything in this company moves at a _____.
5. Are you free for a _____ next Tuesday morning?
6. You and Tom are _____.
7. I'll _____ every week.

Answers

1. traffic jam
2. better late than never
3. impossible to predict
4. snail's pace
5. coffee date
6. in the same boat
7. keep you updated

From Dawn Till Dusk

Eric and Mandy are talking about working a lot.

Eric: How's work going **these days**?

Mandy: The usual. I have to work **from dawn till dusk**. We have all these **strict deadlines** from clients and are always **running out of time**.

Eric: Can you **cut back on** your hours? That's terrible not having any **free time**.

Mandy: Not if I want to **get ahead** in this industry. I'd love to **take my time** on projects. But, that's **not going to cut it**.

Vocabulary

These days: Lately.

From dawn till dusk: Working very long hours (early morning to late at night).

Strict deadlines: A definite time when something needs to be finished.

Running out of time: Lacking time to finish or do something.

Cut back on: Reduce.

Free time: Leisure time when not working or studying.

Get ahead: Make gains, especially compared to other people.

Take my time: Not hurry.

Not going to cut it: Something you do isn't good enough.

Practice

Fill in the blank with the correct word or phrase.

1. Please do it again. That's _____.
2. I hate having to work under _____. It's very stressful.
3. In my _____, I love to hang out with friends.
4. I have to work _____ during the year-end.
5. I'd love to _____ my drinking but it's difficult around the holidays.
6. I'd love to _____ and make a good decision about which program to take.
7. It's difficult to _____ in Vancouver when housing is so expensive.
8. _____, I'm trying to get in better shape.
9. We're _____ and will need to stay late tonight.

Answers

1. not going to cut it
2. strict deadlines
3. free time
4. from dawn till dusk
5. cut back on
6. take my time
7. get ahead
8. these days
9. running out of time

Hit the Sack

Jerry and Larry are talking about being very busy.

Jerry: I have to **hit the sack.** I'm so tired right now.

Larry: Have you been **burning the midnight oil** lately?

Jerry: Yeah, I've been trying to study for this test. I should have started earlier.

Larry: Well, **better late than never**. But, make sure to get enough sleep. If you're tired, you won't remember anything.

Jerry: You're right. It was **many moons** ago that I got a decent night's sleep.

Larry: Don't give up. I think you'll **ace** it.

Jerry: Well, here's hoping I **come up trumps**! Time to **knuckle down** and get to work.

Vocabulary

Hit the sack: Go to bed.

Many moons: A long time ago.

Burning the midnight oil: Staying up late working or studying.

Better late than never: Encouragement after getting a late start to something.

Ace: To get a high mark on a test or do well at something like a job interview.

Come up trumps: To get exactly what is needed at the last minute.

Knuckle down: To focus deeply on something.

Practice

Fill in the blanks with the correct word or phrase.

1. Don't forget to _____ early. It's your big game tomorrow!
2. Although it was _____ ago, I still think about my ex-boyfriend.
3. I've been _____ lately, working a second job.
4. Honestly, it's _____ but he dropped the ball on this project.
5. You won't _____ the test unless you study.
6. That guy has an uncanny ability to always _____.
7. It's the last thing I want to do but I know it's time to _____ and study.

Answers

1. hit the sack
2. many moons
3. burning the midnight oil
4. better late than never
5. ace
6. come up trumps
7. knuckle down

Save me a Seat

Jerry and Sid are talking about coming late to class.

Jerry: Hey Sid, can you **save me a seat** in class? I'm going to **come late**.

Sid: Take your time. I'll even **take notes** for you. But, why are you always late?

Jerry: You know the cute girls always **catch my eye** and then I have to stop and talk. But, **keep up the good work** my friend. I love that you always **pay attention** in class.

Sid: We should **have lunch** after class. What do you think?

Jerry: Sounds great. It's **my treat**.

Vocabulary

Save me a seat: Hold a seat for someone at an event, meeting, class, etc.

Come late: Show up not on time.

Take your time: Don't worry about hurrying.

Take notes: Write down briefly what is being heard.

Catch my eye: Something shiny, sparkling, appealing makes you look.

Keep up the good work: Continue doing the good things you're doing.

Pay attention: Look closely; focus.

Have lunch: Eat lunch.

My treat: I'll pay.

Practice

Fill in the blanks with the correct word or phrase.

1. Do you want to _____ next Friday?
2. Please _____! You'll need to know this for your test next week.
3. If you _____ to Dr. Kim's class, you have to sit in the front row.
4. Jeremy, _____. You did so well on your last report card.
5. Don't worry about it. It's _____.
6. Please _____. I'm going to be a little bit late getting there.
7. I can't go to the mall! So many things _____ and I spend too much money.
8. Please _____ for this meeting, okay?
9. Please _____ doing this test. You have two hours to do it.

Answers

1. have lunch
2. pay attention
3. come late
4. keep up the good work
5. my treat
6. save me a seat
7. catch my eye
8. take notes
9. take your time

At the Farmer's Market

Kerry and Tracy are at the farmer's market.

Kerry: Look how nice these tomatoes are. Should we **pick some out**?

Tracy: Sure. Let's make **bruschetta** tonight for dinner.

Kerry: Perfect. Then we'll need some garlic and basil too. And fresh bread. Let's see if we can find a **baguette**.

Tracy: Definitely. Let's **pick up** some fruit too for lunches. Maybe some peaches or grapes?

Kerry: Okay. I also want to **check out** those cookies and cakes over there.

Tracy: There are so many good things here! I'm happy we decided to come.

Kerry: Me too. Look! Homemade **vegan** samosas. Let's pick up a few of those for tomorrow.

Tracy: Perfect. I hope we have enough bags to carry all of this stuff! We'll be **overloaded**!

Vocabulary

Pick some out: Choose some.

Bruschetta: A kind of snack made with bread, tomatoes, garlic, oil, salt, etc.

Baguette: A long, thin type of bread with a crunchy exterior.

Pick up: Get.

Check out: Have a look at something.

Vegan: Containing no animal products.

Overloaded: More than capacity.

Practice

Fill in the blanks with the correct word or phrase.

1. That boat is _____. Don't you think it might sink?
2. I always order _____ when I go to an Italian restaurant.
3. Let's _____ some sushi for dinner.
4. I'm not sure if that restaurant has any _____ menu items.
5. Let's pick up a fresh _____ to eat with our salad.
6. We should bring flowers tonight. Can you _____?
7. Let's _____ that new restaurant down the street tonight.

Answers

1. overloaded
2. bruschetta
3. pick up
4. vegan
5. baguette
6. pick some out
7. check out

Save the Environment

Keith and Tanya are talking about what they can do to reduce electricity usage.

Tanya: I'm wondering if we can **save money** on our bills and **save the environment** at the same time?

Keith: I don't keep track of the **electricity bill**. Has it gone up?

Tanya: The rates have gone up, yes. I think we can **save electricity** in a few different ways.

Keith: Will it **make a difference**? Aren't things like replacing lightbulbs mostly **a waste of time**?

Tanya: We can **save energy** in several ways. I found this **helpful guide** online. We can try a few of the things in it.

Keith: Okay, let's do it.

Vocabulary

Save money: Have more money in the bank by not wasting money on unnecessary things.

Save the environment: Doing things like recycling, not buying things, reducing food waste.

Electricity bill: How much you pay for electricity each month.

Save electricity/save energy: Doing things like turning off the lights, turning down the heat.

Make a difference: Make an impact with an action you take.

A waste of time: Doing something that is not helpful or doesn't produce results.

Helpful guide: A written document or video that explains in detail how to do something.

Practice

Fill in the blanks with the correct word or phrase.

1. Our _____ is $20 more than normal this month.
2. Small things can add up and _____ for the environment.
3. I want to _____ but I often feel overwhelmed and don't know where to start.
4. Let's try to find a _____ online for how to clean our dishwasher.
5. Don't you think that trying to help him is _____?
6. I'd like to _____ on food by not eating out so much.
7. Let's turn off the lights every morning before we go to work so we can _____.

Answers

1. electricity bill
2. make a difference
3. save the environment
4. helpful guide
5. a waste of time
6. save money
7. save electricity/save energy

Supermarket Strategy

Harry and Mo are deciding on a shopping strategy at the supermarket.

Harry: What do you think? Should we **divide and conquer** or **stick together** this week?

Mo: How much stuff do we need to buy?

Harry: Not that much. Just **the basics**: fruit and vegetables, milk, bread and **a couple of** other things.

Mo: Why don't we stick together then. We'll be **done in a jiffy**.

Harry: Sure, but I get to push the cart, okay? It's my favourite!

Mo: Whatever you want! Here. You hold the list too and cross off the stuff as we buy it.

Harry: Okay. **For the record** though: you're so bossy! I'm not complaining though. I don't want to be the **captain of the ship**!

Vocabulary

Divide and conquer: Each person takes an individual part of a bigger task.

Stick together: Not have differing opinions or actions about something.

The basics: Nothing complicated or excessive.

A couple of: Two

Done in a jiffy: Finishing something quickly.

For the record: Officially.

Captain of the ship: The person in charge of something.

Practice

Fill in the blanks with the correct word or phrase.

1. Let's _____ and we'll finish up more quickly.

2. Let's get _____ of steaks for the BBQ tonight.

3. I know you don't like your boss but someone has to be the _____.

4. We only need _____. It should take just a few minutes.

5. Let's _____ on this decision.

6. _____, I never voted to do this.

7. Stop complaining about your room. You'll be _____ if you just do it.

Answers

1. divide and conquer

2. a couple of

3. captain of the ship

4. the basics

5. stick together

6. for the record

7. done in a jiffy

Eating Habits

Sun and Todd are talking about eating habits.

Sun: Do you have a **New Year's resolution** for 2021?

Todd: A big one! I want to change my **eating habits** by not eating so much **junk food** and **processed food**. I'm going to focus on **home-cooked meals** and smaller **portion sizes**.

Sun: Mine is very similar. I'm not going to **go on a diet** but I want to eat a **balanced diet** with more **fruits and vegetables**. And I want to avoid the **second helpings**, especially at dinner.

Todd: I hope we can do it.

Vocabulary

New Year's resolution: Thing you resolve to do for the upcoming year.

Eating habits: General way of eating (can be healthy or unhealthy).

Junk food: Food that isn't healthy. For example, chips and candy.

Processed food: Food that has been manufactured in some way. Often contains lots of sugar, fat and salt.

Home-cooked meals: Food that you cook at home.

Portion sizes: How much food you eat at one time.

Go on a diet: Eat less or differently to try to lose weight.

Balanced diet: A wide variety of healthy foods.

Fruits and vegetables: Fruits and vegetables!

Second helpings: Taking a second portion of a meal after finishing your first portion.

Practice

Fill in the blanks with the correct word or phrase.

1. My son eats way too much _____. He probably eats an entire box of crackers a day!
2. I want to _____ so that I can lose weight for my sister's wedding.
3. Avoid _____ at dinner if you want to drop a few pounds.
4. I love _____ like potato chips and candy.
5. I want to reduce my _____. For example, only one piece of chicken instead of two.
6. It's best to eat a variety of brightly colored _____.
7. My _____ are terrible. I often skip breakfast and then snack late at night.
8. I love my husband's _____.
9. My _____ is to stop smoking.
10. A _____ consists of healthy foods from a variety of food groups.

Answers

1. processed food
2. go on a diet
3. second helpings
4. junk food
5. portion sizes
6. fruits and vegetables
7. eating habits
8. home-cooked meals
9. New Year's resolution
10. balanced diet

The Last Straw

Bob is talking to Lisa about leaving his wife.

Bob: So I think I'm going to **leave my wife**.

Lisa: On no! What happened? You guys always seemed happy to me.

Bob: Well, **the last straw** was looking at my retirement accounts and seeing that most of them were close to zero. She loves to **shop till she drops** but I didn't realize how bad it was until now.

Lisa: Sorry to hear that. I hope you can get back **in the black**. You went **from rags to riches** once. I'm sure you can do it again.

Bob: Hopefully, but after paying the divorce lawyers, I'll have a lot of work to **make up for lost time** on those retirement accounts. And she may also want **spousal support**.

Lisa: Well, hang in there. I'm here for you.

Vocabulary

The last straw: The final annoying thing before someone loses their patience. For example, a child has been misbehaving all day but his dad finally yelled at him when he wouldn't stay in his room at bedtime.

In the black: To not be in debt.

Leave my wife: Separate or get a divorce.

Shop till she drops: Loves shopping and spends lots of time doing it.

Make up for lost time: Wasted time that you can't get back.

Spousal support: Money paid to a former husband or wife after getting divorced.

From rags to riches: Poor to rich.

Practice

Fill in the blanks with the correct word or phrase.

1. Honestly, this is _____ before he gets fired.
2. We started living frugally and are now _____.
3. I want to _____. We just don't have that much in common anymore.
4. My wife loves to _____ but I feel nervous about how much money she's spending.
5. I had to pay _____ after getting divorced.
6. I only started dating in my twenties. Now, I have to _____.
7. Wow! I love the story of that guy going _____ when he moved to the USA.

Answers

1. the last straw
2. in the black
3. leave my wife
4. shop till she drops
5. spousal support
6. make up for lost time
7. from rags to riches

Buying a New Computer

Keith is shopping for a new computer.

Clerk: Do you need any help finding something?

Keith: I'm looking for a new laptop but I'm **spoiled for choice** here.

Clerk: Sure, I can **help you out**. What did you need it for?

Keith: Basic stuff. Watching Netflix. Online banking. Email and Facebook. **The usual**.

Clerk: Sure, we have some cheaper computers that might be **right up your alley**. Don't **pay top dollar** for these high-end gaming computers.

Keith: That **sounds good** to me. I hate computer games.

Clerk: Okay. Let's **take a look at** some of them.

Vocabulary

Spoiled for choice: A lot of options.

Help you out: Assist.

The usual: The normal thing.

Right up your alley: Something that might be suitable or ideal for you.

Pay top dollar: Spend the maximum amount of money for something.

Sounds good: Great!

Take a look at: Examine.

Practice

Fill in the blanks with the correct word or phrase.

1. You'll be _____ if you go to Old Navy.
2. Yeah, that _____. See you at 6:00.
3. I think that new Italian place will be _____.
4. I can _____ with your homework if you need.
5. I hate to _____ for that kind of thing. The cheaper alternatives work just as well.
6. Let' me _____ your finger. It looks terrible.
7. Oh, _____, please. Just a regular draft beer.

Answers

1. spoiled for choice
2. sounds good
3. right up your alley
4. help you out
5. pay top dollar
6. take a look at
7. the usual

Good With Computers

Sienna is helping Terry with his computer.

Terry: Hey, you're **good with computers**, right? I'm trying to **write an essay** but my **computer freezes** every **couple of minutes**. And then...

Sienna: Did you **shut down your computer** yet?

Terry: No, should I do that?

Sienna: Yes, and then **restart the computer.**

Terry: Okay, it says it's going to do some **scheduled maintenance** and **install updates**.

Sienna: Let that run and once it starts, do a **virus scan**. It should work a lot better now.

Vocabulary

Good with computers: Describes someone who knows how to use computers well.

Write an essay: Write a specific type of school assignment.

Computer freezes: A computer problem where you can't click anything on the screen.

Couple of minutes: Two minutes.

Shut down your computer: Turn off the computer.

Restart the computer: Turn back on the computer after turning it off.

Scheduled maintenance: Routine maintenance that happens on a schedule of some kind.

Install updates: This usually refers to a computer or other electronic device. Involves updating the software.

Virus scan: A program that looks for harmful viruses on a computer.

Practice

1. Let's run a _____ first to see if we can catch any problems that way.

2. Always _____ as soon as possible for your electronic devices to avoid problems.

3. Ted is _____. Let's ask him for some help.

4. I need a _____ to change my clothes before we go.

5. The network will be down for _____ tonight from 2 am to 4 am.

6. Did you _____ your computer yet? I think that might help.

7. I hate that my _____ at the worst possible times.

8. _____ before going home for the day.

9. I have to _____ this weekend. I haven't even started yet.

Answers

1. virus scan

2. install updates

3. good with computers

4. couple of minutes

5. scheduled maintenance

6. restart the computer

7. computer freezes

8. shut down your computer

9. write an essay

Played Soccer

Tom and Jerry are talking about playing soccer.

Tom: What did you get up to **last weekend**?

Jerry: I **played soccer**. We had a match against the **first-place** team in the league. And it was an **away game** too.

Tom: Did you **win the game**?

Jerry: It was **a nail-biter** but we won. The **final score** was 3-2. We were down by two goals but **made a comeback** in the **second half.**

Tom: Congratulations.

Vocabulary

Last weekend: The previous Saturday and Sunday.

Played soccer: Played soccer at some point in the past.

First-place: Top of the league.

Away game: A game that is played on a field that is not your usual play or practice field.

Win the game: Get a higher score than the other team.

Nail-biter: A close game.

Final score: The outcome of a game.

Made a comeback: Came from behind to win.

Second half: The last half of a game.

Practice

Fill in the blank with the correct word or phrase.

1. Hopefully, they'll play better in the _____.
2. We tried to _____ with a final push at the end but ended up tied.
3. Wow! The Yankees _____ in the 9th inning to win it.
4. Who got _____ in the American League?
5. The _____ was 4-3.
6. I _____ almost every day when I was a kid.
7. That game was a serious _____. I had no idea who was going to win.
8. _____, I caught that James Bond movie.
9. Our next _____ is in Toronto next weekend.

Answers

1. second half
2. win the game
3. made a comeback
4. first-place
5. final score
6. played soccer
7. nail-biter
8. last weekend
9. away game

Weekend Plans #1

Sammy and Allan are talking about their weekend plans.

Sammy: What are you up to this weekend?

Allan: Oh, **not much**. I might spend some time getting the garden ready. It's **that time of year**, right?

Sammy: It is for sure. **Spring has sprung**!

Allan: What are you up to?

Sammy: Oh, **nothing really**. Just **hanging out** with my boyfriend. We just **moved in together** so have all kinds of stuff to organize and **tidy up**.

Allan: Oh, that's exciting. When did that happen?

Sammy: Last weekend.

Vocabulary

What are you up to: What's happening lately?

Not much: Almost nothing.

That time of year: The season when something normally happens.

Spring has sprung: An expression you can say when things like flowers and trees start growing again in spring.

Hanging out: Spending time together.

Moved in together: When two people (usually romantic partners) joined households.

Tidy up: Clean; organize.

Practice

Fill in the blanks with the correct word or phrase.

1. _____ these days? Still busy studying?
2. We _____ a couple of years ago now.
3. I need to plant the garden this weekend. It's _____.
4. There's _____ going on these days because of the pandemic.
5. Let's _____ the kitchen before bed.
6. _____. It's going to be 20 degrees this weekend.
7. I love _____ with Tim. He's such a fun guy.

Answers

1. what are you up to
2. moved in together
3. that time of year
4. not much
5. tidy up
6. spring has sprung
7. hanging out

Weekend Plans #2

Jenny and Ted are making some plans for the weekend.

Jenny: Ted, let's hang out this weekend! It's **been a while**.

Ted: I know, right? We haven't hung out in months. I'd love to do something. What do you think?

Jenny: The weather is kind of **iffy** but what about going for a hike? And then we can **grab something to eat** after?

Ted: That's great. Let's go to Mount Seymour. I haven't been there in a long time and it'll be **a piece of cake** even though I'm **out of shape**! **Rain or shine** is good for me.

Jenny: Perfect. I can drive. I'll **pick you up** at 1:00?

Ted: Okay. See you then! I'll bring snacks for us.

Jenny: Perfect.

Vocabulary

Been a while: A moderate length of time

Iffy: Uncertain.

Grab something to eat: Get some food.

A piece of cake: Describes something easy to do.

Out of shape: Not in good health from bad diet or lack of exercise.

Rain or shine: Do something, no matter what the weather is.

Pick you up: Come get you.

Practice

Fill in the blanks with the correct word or phrase.

1. I can _____ around 7:00.
2. The weather looks kind of _____. Why don't we reschedule?
3. Don't worry about that test. It's _____.
4. I'm so _____ these days.
5. It's _____, hasn't it?
6. Why don't we _____ from Subway and take it to the park?
7. I'm planning on going, _____.

Answers

1. pick you up
2. iffy
3. a piece of cake
4. out of shape
5. been a while
6. grab something to eat
7. rain or shine

Bite the Bullet

Jim and Leila are talking about buying a car.

Jim: Hey Linda, so I decided to finally **bite the bullet** and get a new car.

Leila: Oh wow! Did it **break the bank**?

Jim: It was expensive, but I didn't want another **lemon**.

Leila: I know, **when it rains, it pours,** right? Your car was always at the mechanic's shop!

Jim: I know. It was so annoying. Now, I just have to **crack the whip** on my employees to start making more money.

Leila: Don't **discredit** yourself! You're **working your fingers to the bone** too.

Vocabulary

Bite the bullet: Doing something that you've been avoiding for a while. For example, someone finally deciding to paint their house after delaying for years.

When it rains, it pours: When more than one bad thing happens at the same time.

Crack the whip: To be tough on someone.

Break the bank: Something that costs a lot.

A lemon: A reference to a car that needs more repairs than usual.

Discredit: Not give someone credit.

Working your fingers to the bone: Working very hard, beyond capacity.

Practice

Fill in the blanks with the correct word or phrase.

1. I wish he'd just _____ and stop complaining so much!
2. My mom used to _____ and make us all clean the house every Sunday morning.
3. That guy has the worst luck! _____.
4. I hope this new-to-me car I just bought isn't _____.
5. Let's go on a nice vacation but I don't want to _____.
6. I don't want to _____ his success, but his father handed him the job.
7. Take a break Tom! You're _____ lately.

Answers

1. bite the bullet
2. crack the whip
3. When it rain, it pours
4. a lemon
5. break the bank
6. discredit
7. working your fingers to the bone

Doing Chores

Tim and Emily are talking about a plan for cleaning their house.

Tim: Let's get this place **cleaned up**! It's a **pigsty** in here.

Emily: I know. I hate it. Okay, why don't we **put away** all the stuff first? Then it'll be easier to clean.

Tim: Good plan. After that, why don't I **tackle** the bathrooms and you can do the floors.

Emily: Sure. I'll **throw in** a load of laundry first though.

Tim: Okay. Then we can tackle the dusting and clean up the kitchen and whatever else there is to do.

Emily: Uggghhh...this is going to take us so long! Can we try **clean as you go** next month? This is **over the top**.

Vocabulary

Cleaned up: Made not dirty or messy.

Pigsty: Pig's house but refers to a dirty house, room, office, etc.

Put away: Return something to the proper location.

Tackle: Take on.

Throw in: Put something into something.

Clean as you go: A strategy where you clean something immediately after making it dirty or messy.

Over the top: Too much; excessive.

Practice

Fill in the blanks with the correct word or phrase.

1. That guy is _____. I hate running into him at work.
2. Your bedroom is a _____. Clean it up before playing video games.
3. Let's _____ the garage together.
4. If you work in a restaurant, you're expected to _____.
5. Let's _____ all the groceries before we start cooking.
6. I need a few minutes to get _____ before we go.
7. I want to _____ some ice into the cooler before we head out.

Answers

1. over the top
2. pigsty
3. tackle
4. clean as you go
5. put away
6. cleaned up
7. throw in

Surf the Web

Terry and Tom are talking about surfing the Internet.

Terry: Do you want to **grab dinner after work**?

Tom: Sorry, I can't. I have to help my 90-year old grandma **access the Internet**. She **got the Internet hooked up** but can't **surf the web** for some reason.

Terry: That's amazing. My mom barely knows how to **get online** or **check her email** and she's only 60.

Tom: I know, right? Plus she has all sorts of **social media** accounts like *Facebook* and *Pinterest*.

Vocabulary

Grab dinner: Get something to eat for dinner.

After work: When work is done.

Access the Internet: Use the Internet.

Got the Internet hooked up: Get the Internet turned on at home, work, school, etc.

Surf the web: Go online using a web browser.

Get online: Use the Internet.

Check her email: Have a look at an email account.

Social media: Facebook, Pinterest, Twitter, etc.

Practice

Fill in the blanks with the correct word or phrase.

1. What's your favourite _____ platform?
2. _____, I like to go for a run and then go home and cook dinner.
3. She wants to _____ from home as well as at work. Is it possible?
4. I can only _____ at school.
5. What's the best way to _____, phone or computer?
6. Does anyone say _____ these days? Maybe only seniors!
7. Do you want to _____ this weekend?
8. Now that I've _____, I can start online gaming!

Answers

1. social media
2. after work
3. check her email
4. access the Internet
5. get online
6. surf the web
7. grab dinner
8. got the Internet hooked up

How to Split Chores

Bobby and Min are talking about splitting chores.

Bobby: Min, can I talk to you about chores? I'm doing more than my **fair share**. I do all the **meal prep** and laundry and end up doing most of the cleaning too. I sometimes just want to **throw in the towel**.

Min: I know. You're right. I'm sorry. I've been so busy at work that when I get home, I just want to **kick back**. **Many hands make light work**, right?

Bobby: Is there a way to make this fairer?

Min: Why don't we make a chart? I think it'd **work like a charm** for me. Right now, it's just not on my mind. Like every Saturday, I clean the bathrooms. Or, I have to cook dinner on Tuesday and Thursday night.

Bobby: Sure, we can do that.

Min: Thanks for **bringing this up**. I don't want you to feel like you have to do everything.

Vocabulary

Fair share: Equal portion.

Meal prep: The work required to make a meal.

Throw in the towel: Quit.

Kick back: Relax.

Many hands make light work: An idiom that means something isn't a burden if many people help.

Work like a charm: Describes something that would work well.

Bringing this up: Mentioning this.

Practice

Fill in the blanks with the correct word or phrase.

1. I hate _____, but I don't think you paid for your drinks.

2. Billy wants to _____ on soccer, but I told him to give it another month.

3. You know what they say, "_____."

4. Why don't we try one of those _____ boxes next week?

5. I think this new dish soap might _____.

6. I don't mind you choosing what chores you want to do, as long as you do your _____.

7. Summer vacation is here! Let's _____ with some drinks.

Answers

1. bringing this up

2. throw in the towel

3. many hands make light work

4. meal prep

5. work like a charm

6. fair share

7. kick back

Apply for University

Ted and John are talking about what to do after high school.

Ted: Are you in your last year of **high school**?

John: Yes, I'll be finished in a few months from now.

Ted: Congratulations! Did you **apply to university**?

John: Yes, for the University of Toronto. I get **good grades** so I should get in.

Ted: That's great! Did you **choose a major**?

John: Not yet. Everyone does **general studies** in their **first year**. But next year, I want to choose something so I can have a **good salary** when I graduate.

Ted: Good plan.

Vocabulary

High school: Last 3-4 years of school (approximately grades 9-12).

Apply to university: Send in an application to go to university.

Good grades: High marks in classes (mostly A's).

Choose a major: Pick a course of study at university.

Not yet: Not made a decision; haven't done something but plan to in the future.

General studies: Not specific classes.

First year: Year one of something, usually university.

Good salary: Getting paid a lot of money to do a job.

Practice

Fill in the blanks with the correct word or phrase.

1. I don't have to _____ until second year.

2. What _____ did you graduate from?

3. He didn't get _____ so has to retake some classes.

4. I'm planning on taking _____ my first year.

5. The most important thing to me is a job with a _____.

6. I'm in my _____. I just started last month.

7. My son is so lazy that I think he might not even _____.

8. Did you take out the trash? _____.

Answers

1. choose a major

2. high school

3. good grades

4. general studies

5. good salary

6. first year

7. apply to university

8. not yet

No Pain No Gain

Jay and Lily are talking about going back to school.

Jay: I'm thinking about going back to school! **Hitting the books** again. Am I crazy? I haven't been in school for years.

Lily: Well, as I like to say, "**No pain, no gain!**" If you're going to **make some bank** at a new job afterwards, then why not?

Jay: That's what I thought too. I'm going to enjoy the **calm before the storm** though. I'm going to be **as busy as a beaver** once it starts up in September.

Lily: Oh, you'll **weather the storm** just fine. You've got a **good head on your shoulders**. Let's get a beer tonight. You can tell me more about your plan.

Vocabulary

No pain, no gain: Working hard for something.

Calm before the storm: A quiet period before a difficult time period.

Weather the storm: Make it through, or survive a difficult situation.

Hitting the books: Studying.

Make some bank: To earn lots of money.

Good head on your shoulders: Smart/intelligent.

As busy as a beaver: Working a lot or very hard.

Practice

Fill in the blanks with the correct word or phrase.

1. I'm going to work up in northern Canada to _____.
2. Sorry, I can't hang out. I'll be _____ this weekend.
3. I'm just going to enjoy the _____ before things get too crazy at work.
4. I'm trying to get in shape by training for a marathon. It's tough going but _____.
5. You have a _____. You'll be fine at university.
6. It's going to take more than that to _____.
7. He's _____ with that new course he's taking.

Answers

1. make some bank
2. hitting the books
3. calm before the storm
4. no pain, no gain
5. good head on your shoulders
6. weather the storm
7. as busy as a beaver

Vacation Plans

Kevin and Tony are talking about their plans.

Kevin: What are you doing for summer vacation?

Tony: Well, I just **booked off** some time to go camping. I need to **chill out.** I've been **burning the candle at both ends** for months now.

Kevin: I know. You **work like a dog**. Where are you **headed to**?

Tony: To Cultus Lake. It's beautiful there plus there are waterslides for the kids and a pub for me!

Kevin: That sounds just about perfect. I'm going to do a mini **staycation** and do lots of day hikes and stuff like that.

Tony: Sounds nice too. Where do you like hiking?

Kevin: I'm just **getting into it** now. I bought a book though so I'll do some stuff from there.

Vocabulary

Booked off: Submitted a request for time off of work.

Chill out: Relax; take a break.

Burning the candle at both ends: Working many hours, long into the night.

Work like a dog: Working too much to the point of exhaustion.

Headed to: Going.

Staycation: A vacation where you just stay home.

Getting into it: Starting something.

Practice

Fill in the blanks with the correct word or phrase.

1. I'm not sure about tennis yet. I'm just _____.
2. You can't keep _____.
3. Where are you _____ for vacation?
4. I don't want to spend a lot of money. What about a _____?
5. I've _____ the first two weeks of August.
6. I _____ but what do I have to show for it?
7. I plan to just _____ at home this weekend.

Answers

1. getting into it
2. burning the candle at both ends
3. headed to
4. staycation
5. booked off
6. work like a dog
7. chill out

Break a Leg

JT and Lisa are talking about performing in a play.

JT: Hey, I heard **through the grapevine** that you're going to be in a play next month.

Lisa: It's true. I had to **blow off some steam** from work and escaping into my character is a great way to do that.

JT: You're **taking the bull by the horns** lately! Can I come watch?

Lisa: Sure, **knock yourself out**! It's a little bit **amateur hour** but **the price is right**!

JT: Okay, I'll come. I can't forget to tell you to **break a leg** though!

Vocabulary

Break a leg: To wish someone good luck, usually before performing or going on stage.

Blow off some steam: Doing something to get rid of stress. For example, having a few drinks after a difficult work project.

Knock yourself out: To try hard to do something. Often something that others think is a waste of time.

Taking the bull by the horns: Doing something bravely and decisively.

Through the grapevine: To spread information informally. Often related to gossip.

Amateur hour: Not professional.

The price is right: Something is affordably or reasonably priced.

Practice

Fill in the blanks with the correct word or phrase.

1. I heard _____ that Tom and Monica broke up.
2. You want to do that for me? _____.
3. I started playing soccer to _____ from my terrible job.
4. It's not the best quality but _____.
5. Good luck and _____.
6. It was hard to watch that presentation. Talk about _____.
7. I'm _____ at work lately and it's going well!

Answers

1. through the grapevine
2. Knock yourself out
3. blow off some steam
4. the price is right
5. break a leg
6. amateur hour
7. taking the bull by the horns

At the Movie Theater

Peter and Liz are at the movie theater and talking about which movie to see.

Peter: Anything **catch your eye**? Are there any **blockbusters** these days?

Liz: Let's see. What starts around 7:00? Maybe Spiderman or that new drama that everyone is **chewing the fat** about.

Peter: I don't like dramas that much but Spiderman is perfect.

Liz: Okay, it starts in about 10 minutes. That's perfect. Let's get some tickets.

Peter: Sounds good. It's **my treat**! Didn't you buy me dinner last time we hung out?

Liz: I did. Thanks for remembering. Let's **get this show on the road**! The movies start **like clockwork** at this theater. I hate missing the **previews**.

Vocabulary

Catch your eye: Something that seems interesting to you.

Blockbusters: Hit movies.

Chewing the fat: Talking about something.

My treat: I'll pay for it.

Get this show on the road: Begin something.

Like clockwork: On time.

Previews: A teaser about other movies before the movie that you're watching.

Practice

Fill in the blanks with the correct word or phrase.

1. Let's check out the _____ before deciding which one to watch.
2. Are there any _____ in the theaters now?
3. I have no idea what to order. Did anything ____?
4. I'm impatient. Let's _____.
5. I go to bed at 10:00 _____.
6. My dad loves _____ with the neighbors.
7. Let's get dinner tonight. It's _____.

Answers

1. previews
2. blockbusters
3. catch your eye
4. get this show on the road
5. like clockwork
6. chewing the fat
7. my treat

A Suspicious Person

Kerry and Virginia are talking about a suspicious guy in the neighborhood.

Kerry: What's that guy doing? I've seen him **lurking around** here a lot lately.

Virginia: I've seen him around a lot too. Maybe he's planning on **breaking into** Ed and Cindy's house while they're on vacation.

Kerry: Maybe. What should we do?

Virginia: If he does **have sticky fingers**, I think we should call the police. They can come talk to him and **scare him off** hopefully. I'd hate to see Ed and Cindy get **taken to the cleaners**.

Kerry: Okay, I'll give the police **a ring** now.

Virginia: And I'll **keep an eye on** him to see where he goes.

Vocabulary

Lurking around: Spending time in a location, probably not with good intentions.

Breaking into: Entering somewhere without permission.

Have sticky fingers: Likely to steal something.

Scare him off: Warn someone to prevent them from doing something bad.

Taken to the cleaners: Had everything stolen.

A ring: A call.

Keep an eye on: Watch.

Practice

Fill in the blanks with the correct word or phrase.

1. Can you please _____ on Billy while I'm in the shower?

2. Those boys _____. Please don't let them inside the house.

3. Why is that man _____ the neighborhood so much?

4. My friend got _____ by the insurance salesman.

5. I'm going to give your teacher _____ and see if we can figure this out.

6. Joel got caught _____ the convenience store? That's crazy.

7. Make loud noises. Hopefully we can _____.

Answers

1. keep an eye on

2. have sticky fingers

3. lurking around

4. taken to the cleaners

5. a ring

6. breaking into

7. scare him off

You Can't Judge a Book by Its Cover

Jim and Lily are talking about their new neighbor.

Jim: Have you met our new neighbor yet?

Lily: I talked to him last night but he's **a hard nut to crack**. He only gave one-word answers to all my questions!

Jim: Well, **you can't judge a book by its cover**. I'm sure we'll find out more about him as time goes on. Maybe he's not that **talkative.**

Lily: Maybe. But I felt frustrated talking to him for just a few minutes. Anyway, I'm working on not **burning bridges** so I'll keep trying.

Jim: Good plan. You never know **what may come**. Let's invite him over for dinner and see if he **opens up**.

Vocabulary

You can't judge a book by its cover: to not judge something or someone based on appearance. For example, a restaurant that's not stylish and new may have delicious food.

A hard nut to crack: Someone that is difficult to get to know.

Burning bridges: Damaging relationships.

What may come: What could happen in the future.

Talkative: Someone who likes to talk a lot.

Opens up: Shares information about oneself.

Practice

Fill in the blanks with the correct word or phrase.

1. I try my best to avoid _____ when leaving a job.
2. My dad rarely talks and is _____.
3. I learned early on in life that _____.
4. I'm well prepared for _____.
5. My daughter is so _____. I go for a walk every day to get a break!
6. I love it when my son _____ to me. It happens so rarely!

Answers

1. burning bridges
2. a hard nut to crack
3. you can't judge a book by its cover
4. what may come
5. talkative
6. opens up

The New Guy

Eddy and Ethan are talking about a new guy at work.

Eddy: Have you met Bob yet?

Ethan: Oh yeah. He's already kind of **infamous**.

Eddy: I know. He's a weird **dude**. I got a super **bad vibe** from him. We had the strangest conversation about guns at lunch the other day.

Ethan: Same here. I don't have a good feeling about him. He seems pretty **sketchy**.

Eddy: I'm keeping an eye on him for sure.

Ethan: I heard that he's a genius at computer programming though. I guess that's why they **brought him on board**.

Eddy: That must be it. I think he's going to be **a bad egg** here.

Vocabulary

Infamous: Everyone knows about that person or thing.

Dude: Guy.

Bad vibe: Not a good feeling about something or someone.

Sketchy: Not reputable.

Brought him on board: Hired.

Bad egg: A bad person to have on a team or in a company.

Practice

Fill in the blanks with the correct word or phrase.

1. He's a _____ in my class.
2. That _____ is up to no good I think.
3. Why is he acting like that? It's so _____.
4. My sister is _____ at her company for being the one to fire people.
5. I'm so thankful we _____.
6. Did you get a _____ from her as well?

Answers

1. bad egg
2. dude
3. sketchy
4. infamous
5. brought him on board
6. bad vibe

Feeling Under the Weather

Jerry and Linda are talking about not feeling well.

Jerry: My mom used to tell me to not be such a **couch potato** and that **an apple a day keeps the doctor away**. I wish that I'd listened to her! I've been so sick lately.

Linda: I know you're **feeling under the weather** but **this too shall pass.**

Jerry: Thanks Linda, I appreciate you **checking in on** me every day.

Linda: It's the least I can do. You've helped me with so many things over the years. Just don't **kick the bucket** on me, okay?

Vocabulary

Feeling under the weather: Not feeling well; feeling sick.

Couch potato: Someone who spends lots of time on the couch watching TV or movies or playing video games. Not active.

An apple a day keeps the doctor away: Eating healthy keeps you from getting sick.

This too shall pass: A bad time period that will eventually end.

Checking in on: To see how someone is doing.

It's the least I can do: No problem; it's a small thing, usually when you feel like you should do more.

Kick the bucket: Die.

Practice

Fill in the blanks with the correct word or phrase.

1. My dad keeps phoning and _____ me. It's almost too much!
2. I keep nagging my son to get active because he's such a _____.
3. I called in sick because I was feeling a bit _____.
4. I'm convinced that the saying, "_____" does work!
5. My son has been pretty down lately but I told him that, "_____."
6. Lunch is on me. _____, seeing as you've been making me meals all week.
7. I hope that I don't _____ before I'm 80 but I'm nervous about how much I smoke!

Answers

1. checking in on
2. couch potato
3. under the weather
4. An apple a day keeps the doctor away
5. This too shall pass
6. It's the least I can do
7. kick the bucket

Talking About an Accident

Sam and Kerry are talking about an accident.

Sam: Oh Kerry! What happened?

Kerry: I hit a rock while riding my bike and **took a tumble** over the handlebars.

Sam: Oh no! It looks bad.

Kerry: I **got rushed** to ER. I hit my head pretty hard but no **serious damage** because I was wearing a helmet. Just a cut on my leg and some **scrapes** on my hands.

Sam: Thank God for that. How did you not break any bones? You must have **nine lives**.

Kerry: I'm not sure. It's a small **miracle**. They did an x-ray of my entire body to check and I also got a CAT scan of my head which was interesting. They were worried about bleeding in my brain.

Sam: I'm happy to hear that you're okay! You'll be back to your adventure **in no time at all**.

Vocabulary

Took a tumble: Fell off something.

Got rushed: Taken somewhere quickly.

Serious damage: Something bad happened to a person, building, etc.

Scrapes: Small cuts.

Nine lives: A reference to the idiom, "Cats have nine lives," which means that it's impossible to hurt or kill them.

Miracle: Something good that happens but with no reasonable explanation.

In no time at all: Soon; quickly.

Practice

Fill in the blanks with the correct word or phrase

1. If we work together, we'll be done _____.
2. The hurricane caused some _____.
3. That daredevil must have _____.
4. It's a small _____ that he didn't fail the course.
5. My dad _____ to the ER yesterday. It turns out he had a heart attack.
6. My son _____ from the swing and broke his arm.
7. I only have some small _____ and bruises.

Answers

1. in no time at all
2. serious damage
3. nine lives
4. miracle
5. got rushed
6. took a tumble
7. scrapes

Talking About the Weather

Tina and Ed are talking about an upcoming storm.

Tina: Did you see the forecast? They're predicting a **blizzard** for Friday afternoon.

Ed: I heard that. I was thinking about **calling in sick**. I don't want to get caught out in it.

Tina: Same here. The roads will be **treacherous.**

Ed: They definitely will be, especially with the **budget cutbacks**! The city barely has any **snowplows**. It takes them hours to clear even the main roads.

Tina: I know, right? I've noticed that recently too.

Ed: Well, **stay safe** and let me know if you need anything. I have a 4x4 truck so can come rescue you if you need.

Tina: Sure thing. Thank you. I'm **stocked up** on food and water though so I can just stay home.

Vocabulary

Blizzard: A very heavy snowstorm.

Calling in sick: Not going to work because you're "sick."

Treacherous: Extremely dangerous.

Budget cutbacks: When a city, country, or company reduces their spending.

Snowplows: Machines that move snow from roads.

Stay safe: An expression to say when you hope someone can avoid a dangerous situation.

Stocked up: Have lots of supplies.

Practice

Fill in the blanks with the correct word or phrase.

1. Let's get _____ on food and water before the storm hits.
2. They're predicting a huge _____ this weekend.
3. Be careful out there. The icy roads are _____.
4. The _____ mean more students per class.
5. Please _____ and don't take any risks.
6. I'm thinking about _____. I have a bit of a sore throat.
7. The _____ don't get to my neighborhood until days after a storm.

Answers

1. stocked up
2. blizzard
3. treacherous
4. budget cutbacks
5. stay safe
6. calling in sick
7. snowplows

Buttering Me Up

Kerry and Keith are talking about their kids.

Kerry: My kids are **buttering me up** because they don't want to have to help put up **Christmas lights.**

Keith: You're lucky that you can get some help **once in a while**. My kids never **pitch in** for stuff like that.

Kerry: Ah, it's all **smoke and mirrors** at my house usually. My kids **make a show out of** cleaning up after themselves after dinner but their rooms are still like a **pigsty**.

Keith: I know. It's the same for all parents!

Vocabulary

Pitch in: To contribute to or help with something.

Buttering me up: To flatter or please someone because you want something in return. For example, a child who is extra nice to their parents around Christmas because they want an expensive video game system.

Smoke and mirrors: Flashy things that distract from what is real.

Christmas lights: Lights on houses for decoration around Christmas.

Once in a while: Sometimes.

Make a show out of: To do something in a flashy way.

Pigsty: Usually refers to a very messy room or space.

Practice

Fill in the blanks with the correct word or phrase.

1. I like to let loose _____.
2. His presentation was all _____. No real substance.
3. My kids love to help me put up _____.
4. We all _____ every Saturday morning to clean up the house.
5. My kid's bedroom is a _____.
6. I know when my kids are _____ but I fall for it anyway. Their sweet smiles!
7. I hate that my coworkers always _____ finishing even the smallest task.

Answers

1. once in a while
2. smoke and mirrors
3. Christmas lights
4. pitch in
5. pigsty
6. buttering me up
7. make a show out of

Talking About a New Phone

Min-Guy is asking Shuo for some advice about getting a new phone.

Min-Gyu: Hey Shuo, you're **up to date** on the latest technology. I'm thinking about getting a new phone. Can you **lend me a hand**?

Shuo: Ah, what do you have now?

Min-Gyu: An iPhone but it's old and slow now. I want something bigger and better.

Shuo: Are you happy with the iPhone or are you considering switching?

Min-Gyu: Honestly, I'm **ambivalent**. What do you think?

Shuo: Well, the Samsung phones are nice and have **more bang for the buck**. You **pay a premium** for Apple stuff.

Min-Guy: I'm open to switching. Do you have a model recommendation?

Shuo: Let me **look into it** a bit and I'll text you later, okay?

Vocabulary

Up to date: Current.

Lend me a hand: Give me some assistance.

Ambivalent: Don't care either way.

More bang for the buck: A better value.

Pay a premium: Have to pay extra for something, mostly because of the brand name.

Look into it: Find out more information.

Practice

Fill in the blanks with the correct word or phrase

1. I'm not sure yet. I'll have to _____ for you.

2. Please keep your address _____.

3. I'm kind of _____ about whether to go, or not.

4. I don't think we need to _____ for this. There are lots of companies who can do it.

5. Can you _____ with this?

6. We'll get _____ if we hire internally.

Answers

1. look into it

2. up to date

3. ambivalent

4. pay a premium

5. lend me a hand

6. more bang for the buck

Help With Moving

Jenny is helping Tom move.

Tom: Thanks for your help with moving today, Jenny. You **shouldn't have gone to the trouble**.

Jenny: Oh, no problem at all. **I don't mind** helping you. You've been very kind to me over the years. You were so organized, it was **painless**.

Tom: Well, I still appreciate the help.

Jenny: No worries. That's what friends are for.

Tom: What are you doing tomorrow? Let's get dinner. **My treat**.

Jenny: Sure, as long as we get **takeout** and eat in the park. I don't like spending time indoors because of Covid.

Vocabulary

Shouldn't have gone to the trouble: An expression to say when someone has done something extra kind for you.

I don't mind: It's not something that I care about.

Painless: Describes something easy to do.

No worries: No problem at all.

My treat: I'll pay for something.

Takeout: Getting some food from a restaurant to eat outside or at home.

Practice

Fill in the blanks with the correct word or phrase.

1. Let's get some _____ for Jim's birthday and go to the park.
2. You _____. I didn't need a new one!
3. This meeting is going to be annoying, but _____.
4. Let me get it. _____.
5. _____ if you go, or not but I don't plan to.
6. _____ at all. It's not a big deal to me.

Answers

1. takeout
2. shouldn't have gone to the trouble
3. painless
4. my treat
5. I don't mind
6. no worries

Bumping into Someone

Carrie and Tim bumped into each other at the grocery store.

Tim: Carrie!

Carrie: Wow, **it's been a while**, right? Maybe a year?

Tim: Yeah, I think it was around Christmas last year that I **ran into you** at the mall. I was doing my **last-minute shopping**.

Carrie: That's right. **What's up** with you?

Tim: Just busy at work. Not much besides that. How about you?

Carrie: I got a new dog and we've been having so much fun with him.

Tim: Nice! Anyway, nice to see you again! I **gotta run pick up** Tony from soccer pretty soon.

Carrie: For sure. Let's **catch up** over coffee soon.

Vocabulary

It's been a while: Same as, "long time, no see."

Ran into you: Saw in person, randomly.

Last-minute shopping: Going shopping right before you need the present, usually before Christmas.

What's up: What's new?/How are you?

Gotta run: I need to go now.

Pick up: Get something or someone.

Catch up: Share news about what's happening in our lives.

Practice

Fill in the blanks with the correct word or phrase.

1. Let's _____ next week, okay?

2. _____ with you these days?

3. I'm so happy that I _____.

4. I _____. I need to get Tim in 10 minutes.

5. Can you _____ some milk on your way home?

6. Oh wow. _____, hasn't it?

7. I need to do some _____ for the party tomorrow.

Answers

1. catch up

2. what's up

3. ran into you

4. gotta run

5. pick up

6. it's been a while

7. last-minute shopping

The Sleepover

Tim is asking his Mom if he can have a sleepover at his friend's house.

Tim: Hey Mom, can I **stay over** at Tony's house tonight? He just invited me.

Carrie: Are his parents going to be home?

Tim: Of course they are!

Carrie: It is a **school night** though, right? I don't think that's a good idea.

Tim: No, remember it's a holiday tomorrow. It's a **day off** because of parent-teacher interviews.

Carrie: Oh, that's right. I forgot about that. Sure, you can. I'll give his parents **a ring** first though. What time will you go over?

Tim: He said to **come over** for dinner so maybe around 6:00.

Carrie: Okay. I can give you **a lift**.

Vocabulary

Stay over: Sleep at someone's house.

School night: The night before you have to go to school (usually Sunday—Thursday).

Day off: Not working or going to school.

A ring: A phone call.

Come over: Go to someone's house.

A lift: A ride.

Practice

Fill in the blanks with the correct word or phrase.

1. I need _____ to Tony's house, please.
2. You can have the _____ tomorrow. I don't need you.
3. Can I please _____ at Jen's house tonight?
4. Why don't you _____ any time after 7?
5. I have to go to bed at 10:00 on a _____.
6. I'm going to give your teacher _____.

Answers

1. a lift
2. day off
3. stay over
4. come over
5. school night
6. a ring

Before You Go

If you found this book useful, please leave a review wherever you bought it. It will help other English learners, like yourself find this resource.

Printed in Great Britain
by Amazon